Growing Up

A LIFELONG JOURNEY

We have designed *Growing Up: A Lifelong Journey*
to be a shared and prayerful experience.
Each of the eight conversations moves from **Reflection**
to **Conversation** to **Prayer**. Some larger groups will
find it helpful to alternate their weekly discussion
between smaller groups of 2-3 and the larger group
for summarizing discussions. We offer guidance for
weekly Bible reading in preparation for *Conversation
Two* through *Conversation Eight*. We would highly
encourage you to engage in the practice of converting
your thoughts into a written prayer at the end of
each conversation. Be mindful that you are not
talking about God, so to speak, behind his back. Your
conversations with one another include God's loving
and creative presence. May your time together lead to
a deeper discovery and cooperation with God's ongoing
work in this world, in your communities,
and in your lives.

Grace to you and peace
from God our Father
and the Lord Jesus Christ.

Ephesians 1:2

Growing Up

On Growing Up

"...we must grow up in every way into him,
into Christ..."

EPHESIANS 4:15

On Growing Up...

———— ⌘ ————

You stir us to take pleasure in praising you,
because you have made us for yourself,
and our heart is restless until it rests in you.[1]

Augustine
4th Century

I wonder how you would sum up the Christian situation
in the world today. For me, it's a strange, rather tragic,
and disturbing paradox. On the one hand,
in many parts of the world the church is growing
by leaps and bounds. But on the other hand,
throughout the church, superficiality is everywhere.
That's the paradox.
Growth without depth.[2]

John Stott
September 1999

We must no longer be children...But speaking the truth in love,
we must grow up in every way into him who is the head,
into Christ, from whom the whole body,
joined and knitted together by every ligament
with which it is equipped,
as each part is working properly,
promotes the body's growth
in building itself up in love.

Ephesians 4:14-16

———— ⌘ ————

reflection

On the walls and columns of a grey stone sanctuary hung twelve to fifteen prints of Rembrandt's *Return of the Prodigal Son*. Inside, an audience of parents and grandparents, nuns and pastors and students waited expectantly. We were all gathered in a Beverly Hills Anglican church to hear writer/speaker Henri Nouwen speak on his book <u>The Return of the Prodigal Son: A Story of Homecoming</u> (Image Books, 1994). That afternoon over ten years ago, Nouwen beautifully wove together his own life story with the characters of Jesus' Luke 15 parable of the prodigal, the older son and the father, a brief portrait of Rembrandt's life, and the story of the painting. Everyone there was invited into a unique and personal understanding of both sons, and an encounter with the father in this powerful story.

During the question and answer time following Nouwen's presentation, it became clear that the audience identified deeply with the characters' experiences; some knew first-hand the pain of leaving home on bad terms. Others asked questions that revealed the loneliness of sons and daughters who knew only duty in their life of faith. I myself began to ponder the lost-ness of the older son. The bulk of the questions, it seemed, came from concerned moms and dads, who were seeking advice for their children. One of them had a daughter who was much like the younger son in the story. Several had children who "did all the right things." Others had been compelled to kick out a rebellious child. They each were hoping somehow to ensure that their daughters felt loved or their sons did not grow resentful like the older son of the story. What were they to do? They sought direction, assurance, advice. For over thirty minutes, Nouwen replied patiently to each question. He answered each question plainly and directly—except for one.

There is little I recall today of what Nouwen said specifically during the afternoon, except for his answer to that one question. I cannot remember what that mother of a junior high boy asked, but over ten years later, Nouwen's response to her still sticks with me. Instead of explicitly answering her question, he paused, looked intently at the mother and said this:

> *There are a lot of good things that can be said of parenting a child,*
> *but the greatest gift you will give your son is the gift of you being a*
> *growing person yourself.*

We were all "grabbed" by his response. He went on to explain that in a community like a family, love is communicated more by *who you are* than by any single situational choice or strategy. He did not ignore this woman's particular concern for her son, but rather gently enlarged her, and our, perspective. He certainly did not minimize any of those other parenting questions, but in his response he pointed out the critical importance of recognizing the larger canvas upon which life is lived and love is communicated. And in so doing, his words offered far more than parenting advice. As I remember it that afternoon, in his words to this mother, the Spirit seemed to ask all of us: "Are you a growing person?"

Nouwen's words raised for us all the question of spiritual maturity; a large group of adults seemed to look around the room and ask of each other, "Are we still growing up?" Most of the time, this is not a question posed to adults. Rather, it is a framework typically reserved for aunts and uncles, teachers and youth pastors, moms and dads, asked of their children or their students. A grandfather marvels at his grandson, "Boy, have you seen how much so-and-so has grown up?" or a mother bemoans her nineteen year old, "When will so-and-so grow up?" But for adults, the question of whether we are still growing up often goes unasked—perhaps we are assumed to be "grown up" already.

> **Are you a growing person?**

And yet, that afternoon God's Spirit seemed to be poking at this question through Nouwen's words to this concerned mother. *The greatest gift you will give your son is the gift of you being a growing person yourself.* These words continue to echo through my life now fifteen years later. I ask you to let it do some echoing in your life. Do you really *hear* the question? Are you a growing person?

Almost 2000 years ago, the Apostle Paul wrote a letter that undoubtedly prompted pause, reflection, and prayer for any number of believers in and around the large commercial city of Ephesus. For a particular group of believers who struggled with fear, disunity, and immorality, Paul's words brought both support and challenge to their entire way of life. After painting a magnificent portrait of God at work in the world through Christ (Ephesians 1-3), Paul urged the believers to live a way of life worthy of God's gracious and powerful work (4:1). He leaned into their fearful lives and challenged them to mature as persons. Paul wrote,

> *We must not longer be children…But speaking the truth in love, we must grow up in every way into him who is the head, into Christ, from whom the whole body, joined and knitted together by every ligament with which it is equipped, as each part is working properly, promotes the body's growth in building itself up in love. (Ephesians 4:14-16)*

Followers of Jesus Christ over the centuries have continued to encounter Paul's challenge to the believers in Ephesus. Men and women who have confessed faith in Jesus have discovered their lives to be too often fearful, preoccupied, and immature well into their faith journeys. And it has been amidst these hard discoveries along the way that they have graciously encountered the Spirit of God patiently inviting them afresh *to grow up in every way into Christ.* As we stand today in the wake of this long line of believers, we must discover yet again in the everydayness of our lives that growing up into Christ is a lifelong journey.

So let us look around the room and ask of each other and ourselves honestly; where are we on this journey? Amidst all the demands and joys, the activities and expectations of our lives currently, are we *growing up as people?* In what ways is the Spirit of God inviting us to deeper maturity in Christ?

conversation

New discoveries can be made when we can talk to one another in the spirit and company of friendship. Good conversation requires *deep listening* and *honest dialogue*. And certainly with the hurried and hectic pace of life we could use a little more of both. We invite you to enter some good conversation through the questions below. Listen for new questions and perspectives emerging from your time together. Allow this to be a gift of space for one another.

• What stood out to you from the above reflection?

• Where have you observed a need for depth?

• What do *you* think it means to be a growing person? Who has been a growing person in your life?

prayer

What has this reflection and conversation stirred in your mind and heart? Convert your thoughts and feelings into a written prayer:

My prayer is that God's work of creation may continue in me
as well as in my plants, that my soul
may become his garden,
whether a place of wild and spontaneous beauty
like a mountainside—part of the green wilderness—or a more
gentle work of God's art,
in a sheltered garden with a diversity of colors and shapes,
only God can determine; he loves green,
and the growth it signals,
in any setting. But I have faith that in my life he will see
continued evidence of his loving cultivation...

I pray that my Creator will give me "eyes to see" and a gift of
attentiveness and awareness to his smallest details,
which are signals of love and care....

That if I am wilting or barren, unable to produce flowers or fruit,
he will supply me with the kind of fertilizer that encourages
growth without burning the plant.

That if I need the kind of tender, daily, loving care that I give
to my houseplants, God will reassure me that
I am a plant in his house.

That I may be able to relinquish control over my garden,
yielding it into hands of the Gardener
who has my best intentions at heart,
who knows how to use my personal colors and
growth patterns to his own glory. Amen.[3]

Luci Shaw, poet

GROWING UP TOGETHER...

We all could use some time for pause and reflection
along the way of learning to follow Jesus. Let this
question of growth be an opportunity for us to pause,
reflect, and pray together over the next several weeks.
We will launch our *Growing Up* conversations together
around three defining questions for the journey:

- *Who is God?*
- *Who am I?*
- *What am I to do with my life?*

We never grow out of these questions along the way of
following Jesus. Rather we grow into them. Our hope
is that these next several weeks will serve to personally
deepen our attentiveness and responsiveness to God's
gracious and maturing work among us. In the name of
Jesus.

——————— ❦ ———————

Throughout this week: Read and reflect upon Ephesians
1:1-22, asking yourself the question: *What are Paul's
deep concerns for the believers in Ephesus?*

Who Is God?

Knowing God

Knowing God

PREPARATION: Read and reflect upon Ephesians 1:1-22, asking the question: *What are Paul's deep concerns for the believers in Ephesus?*

——————— ❦ ———————

The truth is that the term spiritual life *is simply a way of referring to one's life—*
every moment and facet of it—from God's perspective.
Another way of saying it is this:
God is not interested in your "spiritual life."
God is interested in your life. He intends to redeem it.[4]

John Ortberg

For many of us, our engagement with the Christian faith
is somewhat superficial. At least, that is what I found
about my own faith. I had given much time to trying to understand
the basic ideas of the Christian faith and
appreciating the wonderful way in which those ideas interlock.
I had gained a lot from grasping the wonderful coherence of Christian doctrine.
Yet, at times, this seemed to be little more than just kicking ideas around.
It was as if there were one part of my life that dealt with ideas,
and this somehow never seemed to come into contact with anything else.
It began to seem unreal and irrelevant. As I wrestled with this, I began to realize
that my faith was actually quite superficial.
I had understood *things, but had failed to* appreciate *them.*[5]

Alister McGrath

Blessed be the God and Father of our Lord Jesus Christ,
who has blessed us in Christ
with every spiritual blessing in the heavenly places.

Ephesians 1:3

——————— ❦ ———————

reflection

J.I. Packer begins his classic book <u>Knowing God</u> by pointing out two distinct pathways we can take in the journey of knowing God. He borrows an illustration in order to highlight the contrast between the two. Packer writes,

> *In* A Preface to Christian Theology, *John Mackay illustrated two kinds of interest in Christian things by picturing persons sitting on the high front balcony of a Spanish house watching travelers go by on the road below. The "balconeers" can overhear the travelers' talk and chat with them; they may comment critically on the way that the travelers walk; or they may discuss questions about the road, how it can exist at all or lead anywhere, what might be seen from different points along it, and so forth; but they are onlookers, and their problems are theoretical only. The travelers, by contrast, face problems which, though they have their theoretical angle, are essentially practical—problems of the "which-way-to-go" and "how-to-make-it" type, problems which call not merely for comprehension but for decision and action, too.*
>
> *Balconeers and travelers may think over the same area, yet their problems differ.[6]*

Picture these persons in your mind—the balconeers and the travelers. Notice how their vastly different perspectives affect not only their perceptions and conversations, but their decisions and actions as well—or the lack thereof. We are *travelers* together on this lifelong journey of *growing up into Christ* and as such we must approach our defining questions—Who is God? Who am I? What am I to do with my life?—as travelers, not merely as detached balconeers. We do not stand aloof, observing God's work in the world as spectators. Rather we seek to *know* God, as active participants in this God-given life together.

Where would you place yourself today in this illustration? Are you seated in the balcony or traveling on the road? There is tremendous pressure in our lives and even our churches to keep our knowing of God restricted to the balcony level; we spend a lot of time discussing good ideas or correct doctrine about God, and with good reason. Ideas and concepts certainly have a necessary and critical place in knowing God. But we travelers must not be fooled into thinking we will reach maturity in Christ just by "kicking the right ideas around." One can have the correct answers to all sorts of biblical questions, yet live miserably. One can know a lot about God, yet not want to be personally involved with God. Eugene Peterson captures the importance of a traveler's perspective on knowing God this way;

> In long retrospect over the Jewish and Christian centuries, it's no exaggeration to say that anything we know about God that's not prayed soon turns bad. The name of God without prayer to God is the stuff of blasphemy. The truth about God without love for God quickly becomes oppression. So-called theologians, whether amateur or professional, who don't pray are in league with the devil. Indeed, the devil can be defined as that species of theologian who knows everything about God but will have nothing to do with him.[7]

The process by which we endeavor to know God must be practical and prayerful. As travelers together, let's allow the Holy Spirit to move us beyond the balcony and its theoretical discussions, borrowed convictions, and second-hand experiences of God.

———— ✻ ————

I ask—ask the God of our Master, Jesus Christ, the God of glory—to make you intelligent and discerning in knowing him personally, your eyes focused and clear, so that you can see exactly what it is he is calling you to do, grasp the immensity of this glorious way of life he has for Christians, oh, the utter extravagance of his work in us who trust him—endless energy, boundless strength!

Apostle Paul
Ephesians 1:17-19
The Message

———— ✻ ————

God is up to something good in this world, in our communities, and in our unique lives. This guiding assumption must increasingly challenge all our thinking and living along the way. The testimony of the Scriptures is very clear. Our burden is not primarily to get God to do something good, as if God was reluctant or disinterested. Instead, our responsibility is to cultivate deep attention to the work God is already doing. Creating. Saving. Building community. These are not abstract concepts; rather, they are ongoing God-realities in this world, in our communities, and in our lives. We are immersed in God's creative, redemptive, and saving work in this world, but are we growing in our attentiveness to it? Are we learning to see and understand and trust God's gracious presence and activity among us?

This assumption is basic to our maturity. Growing up into Christ is about cultivating an ongoing and prayerful *(i) attention* to God's gracious way in the world, and *(ii) alignment* of our lives with God's gracious way. For invariably, it is out of our growing attentiveness to God's presence and activity that we will find ourselves being invited by the Holy Spirit to cooperate and align our lives with God's work and way in the world.

God is up to something good in this world, in our communities, and in our unique lives. But, admittedly, sometimes it is hard to see this amidst the everydayness of newspaper headlines and school plays, supermarkets and quarterly forecasts, famines and fast food. We need some help in seeing this because this guiding assumption challenges so much of the prevailing cultural wisdom that relegates God to the edges of our attention.

Like us, the believers in Ephesus also needed some help in keeping God central to their attention. Amidst the many cultural challenges they faced, Paul urged the believers in Ephesus to pay attention to the magnificent work God was— and is—up to in Christ. He sought to encourage ongoing *attention* and *alignment*

> **Growing up into Christ is about cultivating an ongoing and prayerful *(i) attention* to God's gracious way in the world, and *(ii) alignment* of our lives with God's gracious way.**

to God's way by offering a portrait of God's work in the world throughout history with Jesus as its focal point. God is up to something very good, and this "something good" is intimately connected to Jesus. As fellow *travelers* who also need help cultivating God-attention and God-alignment along our life journeys, we would do well to listen in on Paul's words to the believers in Ephesus:

> *I pray for you constantly, asking God, the glorious Father of our Lord Jesus Christ, to give you spiritual wisdom and insight so that you might grow in your knowledge of God. I pray that your hearts will be flooded with light so that you can understand the confident hope he has given to those he called—his holy people who are his rich and glorious inheritance.*

> *Ephesians 1:16b-18*
> New Living Translation

conversation

New discoveries can be made when we can talk to one another in the spirit and company of friendship. Good conversation requires *deep listening* and *honest dialogue*. We invite you to enter into some good conversation by way of the questions below. Listen for new questions and perspectives emerging from your time together. May our listening together invite a deeper understanding and appreciation for who God is.

• What stood out to you from the above reflection?

• How is it possible to know a lot about God and the Bible and yet not really be personally involved with God?

• In Ephesians 1, what does it seem that Paul wants the believers to pay attention to and appreciate?

• Where in your life are you being invited to more deeply *pay attention*?

prayer

What has this reflection and conversation stirred in your mind and heart? Convert your thoughts and feelings into a written prayer:

In your presence we become aware
of how little we know of ourselves,
of our interests and passions,
of our fears and dreads,
of our wonderments and gifts.
In your truthfulness, let us know more of you
and in knowing you, ourselves as well.
We pray in the name of Jesus, where we can see you fully,
and ourselves clearly.
Amen.[8]

Walter Brueggemann

GROWING UP TOGETHER...

In preparation for next week's conversation, read and reflect upon Ephesians 2:1-10, asking the question: *What is God up to in the world according to Paul?*

Who Is God?

Sharing God's Life

Sharing God's Life

PREPARATION: Read and reflect upon Ephesians 2:1-10, asking the question: *What is God up to in the world according to Paul?*

———— ✺ ————

Now the whole offer which Christianity makes is this:
that we can, if we let God have His way, come to share in the life of Christ....
He came to this world and became man in order to spread to other men
the kind of life He has—by what I call a "good infection."[9]

C.S. Lewis

It wasn't so long ago that you were mired in that old stagnant life of sin.
You let the world, which doesn't know the first thing about living,
tell you how to live....It's a wonder God didn't lose his temper
and do away with the whole lot of us.
Instead, immense in mercy, and with incredible love, he embraced us.

Ephesians 2:1, 4
The Message

The centrality of grace combines with the centrality of Jesus.
What Jesus did in his life, death, resurrection makes grace available;
and we receive it through seeking a living relationship with him.
Because salvation promises as its fulfillment
a perfectly restored relationship with God,
it makes sense that this can be achieved only through relationship.
Not through a set of rules or practices, a social system,
or a philosophy but through recentering one's life on a person.[10]

Debra Rienstra

———— ✺ ————

reflection

God is up to something good in this world, in our communities, and in our unique lives. One way of describing Christian maturity is to say that it is the lifelong process by which our lives and our stories become centered in God's life and God's good story.

It is a wonderful day when we come to know that God has entered our story. How transforming to recognize such a personal and loving presence within our lives! It changes our whole way of being in the world. Nothing looks the same.

But this is not the only such discovery along the journey. It is perhaps even more momentous when we see that not only is God part of our story, but that we are actually part of God's story; his unfolding narrative and work in this world. Again, this gracious discovery confronts and deepens our whole way of seeing and being in the world. God is up to something very good. And we are not spectators. We are participants in this work.

Or, put another way, there are two very significant awakenings in our growing up into Christ: (1) When we first realize that God has entered our lives, and (2) *sometimes years later*, when we realize that *we* have entered *God's* life. For some of us it is not until well down the road that we come to appreciate that God's concern and commitment extends far beyond simply making our lives better (which he certainly does!). His intentions are much more than an improvement plan for our individual lives. He wants to share his very life and work with us.

Consider for a moment, or perhaps *reconsider*, the early wisdom we received as children in Sunday school, where we were introduced to God's life as a sort of family life. As we learned all those years ago, God is introducing us into the way of his *family*. We come along like orphans, without siblings or parents, without direction, without guidance, but with a desperate need to be "familied." We are invited to be members of God's family life. The Father of the Lord Jesus is "re-parenting" us by the

Spirit. Jesus is "re-brothering" us by the Spirit. We are learning to be sons and daughters of God.

And in truth this is what the Spirit does—he "families" orphans. Whether or not we are fully aware of it, we long for the attention and the discipline and the *rootedness* of this family. We have tried making it on our own, but there is a growing sense that we have been made for a shared life; the sort of shared life that seems to resonate from this family of Father, Son, and Spirit. Then comes the wonderful discovery: God is taking a particular interest in *us*. The family of God is entering into *our* orphaned life. This new family pays attention to us. We are invited to family gatherings, birthdays and holidays, where there is feasting and laughter and gifts. The attention fills a spot that has been aching for years. It seems to make so much sense of our life that didn't make sense before. This is what we have been missing.

But the life of the orphan does not shrug off easily. In time we begin to recognize that some of the old aches and questions and loneliness remain. In truth, we hear the Father's words of affirmation and attention, but we are still reluctant. We show up at all the gatherings, we accept the gifts, but we're not fully comfortable with this strangely shared community. That is, does this family really desire us to be a part? All this attention might in fact be too good to be true. We wait for an angle, a catch, another shoe to drop. Loneliness is far more familiar to us than this new family.

> God decided in advance to adopt us into his own family by bringing us to himself through Jesus Christ. This is what he wanted to do, and it gave him great pleasure.
>
> Ephesians 1:5
> *New Living Translation*

Even in the presence of genuine love, orphans often hold onto the isolated life that they know and understand. So too we hold a portion of ourselves back. We experience the family on our terms, all the while suspicious as to whether we really belong here, for we cannot really imagine ourselves as actual brothers or sisters, sons or daughters.

The love of the family certainly has changed us, but we continue to resist full immersion into its shared life.

Such is the struggle in many of our lives of faith. We are keenly aware that God has entered our lives, but we are ignorant and even resistant to the reality that we have entered God's life. We hold onto our individual way of seeing and being in the world. So as we grow up into Christ, we must expect a deep inner struggle between our former life, understood and lived individually, and our new life, shared in Jesus.

It is at this critical juncture that we need help in recognizing this, that we need *friends*, other brothers and sisters, who will consistently challenge our individual and "orphaned" ways of being in the world; who will remind us, at difficult times, that we have not been abandoned. We need others who will remind and reassure us that God is re-parenting us, converting our whole way in the world, and lovingly shaping us into a more holy and human form. And somehow and somewhere, surrounded by these gracious reminders, we wake again and again to the startling reality that our life and work is found within God's generous life and work and way.

———— ⟲⟳ ————

Now God has us where he wants us, with all the time in this world
and the next to shower grace and kindness upon us in Christ Jesus.
Saving us is all his idea, and all his work. All we do is trust him
enough to let him do it.
It's God's gift from start to finish!

Ephesians 2: 7-8a
The Message

———— ⟲⟳ ————

May our attention and trust in this deeply generous life of God grow. In Jesus' name.

conversation

Good conversation requires *deep listening* and *honest dialogue*. We invite you to continue some good conversation through the questions below. Listen for new questions and perspectives emerging from your time together. May our listening together invite a deeper understanding and appreciation for who God is and who we are.

• What stood out to you from the above reflection?

• How does it change your thinking and living to realize that not only has God entered your life, but he has invited you to enter his life?

• How have you been reminded over the past few years that God takes a particular and loving pleasure in who you are? What hinders you from fully accepting and appreciating God's love for you?

• In what ways do you find yourself needing to be "re-parented" by God? What must be learned, as well as unlearned?

prayer

What has this reflection and conversation stirred in your mind and heart? Convert your thoughts and feelings into a written prayer:

———— ⚜ ————

God, giver of life
you alone know
how our life can truly succeed....
Show us how to let go
of whatever hinders us
from meeting you,
from letting ourselves be touched by your Word.
Help us to welcome and accept
whatever in us yearns to come alive
in the image and likeness
you have dreamed for us today
and every day for ever and ever.[11]

Amen.

———— ⚜ ————

GROWING UP TOGETHER...

In preparation for next week's conversation read and reflect upon Ephesians 2:1-3:21, asking again the question: *What is God up to?*

Who Am I?

What's defining you nowadays?

What's Defining
You Nowadays?

PREPARATION: Read and reflect upon Ephesians 2:1-3:21, asking the question: *What is God up to?*

———————— ❦ ————————

*Although we speak of certain people as being self-made,
no one is truly their own creation. Personhood is not an accomplishment;
it is a gift....our true self—the self we are becoming in God—is something
we receive from God. Any other identity is of our own making
and is an illusion.*[12]

David Benner

*We too often feel that God's love for us is conditional
like our love is for others. We have made God in our image
rather than seeing ourselves in God's image.
We have belittled God's love and turned our lives
into an endless attempt to prove our worth.
Ours is a culture of achievement, and we carry over these attitudes
to our relationship with God. We work ourselves to a frazzle
trying to impress everyone including God. We try to earn
God's approval and acceptance. We cannot believe
that our relationship with God,
our standing before God,
has got nothing to do with our performance.*[13]

Desmond Tutu

*And what do you benefit if you gain the whole world
but are yourself lost or destroyed?*

Luke 9:25
The New Living Translation

———————— ❦ ————————

reflection

So what's defining you nowadays?

God is profoundly concerned with who you understand yourself to be. He takes great pleasure in our discovery of who we truly are. And, in this regard, we have a lot of learning, as well as unlearning, to do along the way.

For we experience a great deal of personal suffering and confusion in life because we have not come to understand who we really are. We are like the orphans mentioned in our earlier conversation, struggling to trust the love of the adopting family. Just as they cling to the familiarity of their orphaned way of life, so also do we cling to our false understandings of who we are.

Spiritual writer Henri Nouwen pointed out that we learn to identify ourselves in our culture—or put another way, to answer the question "Who am I?"—in one or a combination of the following ways:

> *I am what I do.*
> *I am what others say about me.*
> *I am what I have.*

By the time we reach adulthood, one of these three defining themes tends to dominate our lives. Let's reflect upon each of these in more detail. Pay attention to which of the three seems to correlate most closely to your life experience.

I am what I do. Many of us learn early on in life to define ourselves by our competencies and accomplishments and functions. When we were young we dreamt of all the things we hoped to do some day. When we became old we pointed to the trophies on our shelves, the projects completed, and the pictures of the children we had raised, and recalled all that we had done in our lives. In between, perhaps without our even noticing, a life has been shaped in which our happiness is dependent upon our success or failure to achieve whatever we set out to do.

I am what others say about me. Some of us grow up keenly attuned and attached to peoples' perceptions and expectations of us. Affirmation and rejection are extremely powerful, even controlling forces in our hearts. They can drive us for years—and sometimes even decades. A sort of harmony and/or popularity can become our sought-after goal in every situation. Our lives over the years are motivated or debilitated, whatever the case may be, by the opinions of those who surround us. If someone speaks well of us we are content; but if someone speaks ill of us we are restless, chased by their unmet expectations.

I am what I have. For others of us, what we possess becomes deeply integral to who we are. We can *have* all sorts of things that define us. These can be material in nature, but they don't have to be. We can possess cars, houses, and other "stuff," but we also can have families or jobs or personalities or influence, which we mistakenly believe define us at the core. In each case, we seek to establish who we are by what we possess. The loss of any of these things can be devastating to our core identity as persons.

Throughout our lives we expend a lot of energy trying to prove our worth; trying to secure love or significance in one of those three ways. That said, nothing is intrinsically wrong with *what I do* or *what others say about me* or *what I have*. Achievement and reputation and influence have their good and proper place in our lives. But when any of these occupy the core of our identity, our lives are perched on rickety scaffolding. Why? Because these are not who we are at the core! The core of a person's identity can be defined as the central essence to which one feels attached, which in turn provides motivation for decisions and actions. All of these ways of identifying ourselves are insufficient in defining our core identity. We are more than the sum of these parts—what we do or what others say about us or what we have. God has a much more intimate and personally involving definition in mind. In truth, we had already been defined long before any of these things had come to be.

Who am I? We are God's unique and beloved children by his creative and gracious design. God created and established us in love, and God patiently matures us in love by the Holy Spirit. The Apostle Paul reached out to the believers in Ephesus and impressed upon them this thoroughly relational reality. He told them that through relationship to Jesus they were now God's *children* adopted and loved into the family (1:5), having received *a family inheritance* with the Holy Spirit as the down payment (1:11-14). Who we are is inextricably grafted to who God is. And Paul wanted the believers to understand and appreciate that loving reality in the very depths of their being. Listen to the passion and concern of his prayer.

> *I pray that from his glorious, unlimited resources he will empower you with inner strength through his Spirit. Then Christ will make his home in your hearts as you trust in him. Your roots will grow down into God's love and keep you strong. And may you have the power to understand, as all God's people should, how wide, how long, how high, and how deep his love is. May you experience the love of Christ, though it is too great to understand fully. Then you will be made complete with all the fullness of life and power that comes from God. (3:16-19 NLT)*

Paul's words continue to reach out across the centuries to remind us that God is profoundly concerned with who we understand ourselves to be. We are God's beloved people—his children.

A North African pastor over fifteen hundred years ago named Augustine encouraged his congregation to grow up into this stunning God-reality when he prayed, "You stir us to take pleasure in praising you, because you have made us for yourself, and our heart is restless until it rests in you." Growing up into who we truly are is quite a long, and sometimes difficult, journey. And along the way it is so easy to resist our true identity, or exchange it for the pale imitations offered in today's world. There are so many defining voices seducing us into a misunderstanding of who we are. We need much help from our brothers and sisters in Christ, who can remind us of who we really are. It is a good thing from time to time to reflect upon the ways in which we are each *restless*; and that we struggle to find our rest in God. May our conversation together lead to a deeper discovery of our way of life as beloved sons and daughters of God in this world.

conversation

Good conversation requires *deep listening* and *honest dialogue*. We invite you to continue some good conversation through the questions below. Listen for new questions and perspectives emerging from your time together. May our listening together invite a deeper understanding and appreciation for who God is and who we are.

• What stood out to you from the above reflection?

• As you look back over the ways you have tended to define yourself, which of these themes most resonates with you?

...I am what I do (e.g. achievement, competencies, function)

...I am what others say of me (e.g. popularity, reputation)

...I am what I have (e.g. power, personality, family, things)

• Augustine prays, "You have made us for yourself, and our heart is restless until it finds its rest in you." What sort of restlessness are you currently experiencing in your life?

• How can we help one another more deeply recognize and embrace our identities as beloved children of God?

prayer

What has this reflection and conversation stirred in your mind and heart? Convert your thoughts and feelings into a written prayer:

Who am I? This or the other?
Am I one person today and tomorrow another?
Am I both at once? A hypocrite before others,
And before myself a contemptibly woebegone weakling?
Or is something within me still like a beaten army,
Fleeing in disorder from victory already achieved?
Who am I? They mock me, these lonely questions of mine.
Whoever I am, Thou knowest, O God, I am Thine![14]

Dietrich Bonhoeffer (1906-1945)

(This prayer was penned while Bonhoeffer was imprisoned in a Nazi prison camp.)

GROWING UP TOGETHER...

In preparation for next week's conversation read and reflect upon Psalm 139, asking again the question: *What is God up to?*

Who Am I?

Psalm 139

Psalm 139

PREPARATION: Read and reflect upon Psalm 139, asking the question: *What is God up to?*

——————   ❧   ——————

O Lord, you have searched me and known me.

Psalm 139:1
(NRSV)

Nearly all the wisdom we possess, that is to say, true and sound wisdom,
consists of two parts: the knowledge of God and of ourselves.
But, while joined by many bonds,
which one precedes and brings forth the other is not easy to discern.[16]

John Calvin

[Grace] is unearned love—the love that goes before,
that greets us on the way. It's the help you receive
when you have no bright ideas left,
when you are empty and desperate and have discovered
that your best thinking and most charming charm have failed you.
Grace is the light or electricity or juice or breeze
that takes you from that isolated place
and puts you with others who are as startled and embarrassed
and eventually grateful as you are to be there.[17]

Anne Lamott

——————   ❧   ——————

reflection

It was on a Saturday afternoon in late January over twenty years ago that a high school senior sat down at his kitchen table to complete his final college application. He had every intention of rushing through this application that afternoon. But the fourth essay question slowed him down a good bit. Essay question #4 went like this:

> *Imagine it is your 70th year and you have just completed your 457-page autobiography. Please submit page 221.*

The *difficulty* of the question stopped the young man in his tracks that day. He languished through a long afternoon as he struggled to imagine his page 221. While the difficulty unnerved him in the moment, the *creativity* of the question marked his memory for the rest of his life. *My life is a story.* Up until that moment he had never really imagined his life, or anyone else's life for that matter, as a story.

> *What would you put on page 221 of your 457-page life story?*

This "story" framework offers more than just a clever way to describe our lives. In actuality, story is the way "experience presents itself to us"[18] in everyday life. And realizing this can help us make sense of our unfolding lives. In his book <u>Epic: The Story God Is Telling</u>, John Eldredge describes it this way,

> *I expect all of us, at one time or another, in an attempt to understand our lives or discover what we ought to do, have gone to someone else with our stories. This is not merely the province of psychotherapists or priests, but of any good friend. "Tell me what happened. Tell me your story, and I'll try to help you make sense of it."*

> *You seem...stuck. Things fall apart. What does it all mean? Should you have chosen a different major after all? Were you meant to take that teaching job? Are you going to find someone to*

spend your life with, and will he or she remain true? What about the kids—are they headed in the right direction? Did you miss an opportunity in their lives, some key moment along the way? And if crucial moments are about to happen, will you recognize them? Will you miss your cues?

We humans share these lingering questions: "Who am I really? Why am I here? Where will I find life? What does God want of me?" The answers to these questions seem to come only when we know the rest of the story.[19]

Each of us has a unique story. Or, if you like, each of us *is* a unique story. And our unique stories matter deeply to God. This startling reality demands our thoughtful attention as we consider Psalm 139: a first person testimony of what God is like. God creates and forgives and shapes and loves us *particularly*. He actually cares about our individual lives.

> **The assumption of [Christian] spirituality is that always God is doing something before I know it. So the task is not to get God to do something I think needs to be done, but to become aware of what God is doing so that I can respond to it and participate and take delight in it.[20]**
>
> **Eugene Peterson**

In Psalm 139, David's prayer invites us into a conversation with God—a Person who is beyond anyone or anything he can imagine. David is confronted with a Person who is all-knowing (vv.1-6), who is all-present (vv.7-12), and who is the source of his own personhood (vv.13-18). God's knowledge and presence are neither impersonal nor distant: David addresses God particularly and personally—as "you." And it is clear that God's thoughts of David are not general either. They are particular thoughts, unique to David, and they astonish him. David cries out, "Such knowledge is too wonderful for me/ it is so high that I cannot attain it" (v.6). And again, "How weighty to me are your thoughts, O God!/ How vast is the sum of them!/ I try to count them—they are more than the sand;/ I come to the end—I am still with you" (vv.17-18). Pause for a moment and think on this: do you recognize that this is the sort of Person with whom you are in relationship? Or, at the very least, that this Person is deeply acquainted with you? We have been shaped and formed by a God who knows us and loves us infinitely and particularly.

For many of us, our growing up into Christ has been stunted because we have failed to recognize and appreciate God's shaping hand throughout our *whole* story. We tend to restrict our God-attention to only certain parts of our lives that fit comfortably with our definitions of growth. We avoid the past and sugarcoat the present in our efforts for a better future. We look for God where we expect God to be—in church, at weddings, baptisms and the like. It is difficult to imagine that God could be present with us in times of failure or questioning; in moments of pain or rebellion. But God *is* and *has been* graciously present all along. God uses the entire landscape of our lives to craft and mature us—the good, the bad and the ugly of our stories.

*God is up to something good and has been up to something good...*Where has God's grace been operating all along the way of our life stories? Writer Annie Dillard has insisted that we become "detectives of divinity." We need help and courage in *seeing God's grace-at-work* in our lives and in our communities. For it sometimes is found in the most unlikely of places. As David cries out to God, "Even the darkness is not dark to you; the night is as bright as the day, for darkness is as light to you" (Psalm 139:12, ESV). God is a wondrously creative Being who weaves together all the "stuff" of our lives into a more holy and human shape. Looking back on the particular characters and circumstances of our lives can help us see more clearly and trust more deeply God's loving activity among us.

Our life stories matter immensely to God. We would each do well to prayerfully reflect upon the ways God has been nurturing and shaping us over the course of our lives. How is it that you have seen God's grace operating in your life? What is your story to tell?

conversation

Good conversation requires *deep listening* and *honest dialogue*. We invite you to continue some good conversation through the questions below. Listen for new questions and perspectives emerging from your time together. May our listening together invite a deeper understanding and appreciation for who God is and who we are.

• What stood out to you from the above reflection?

GRACE-AT-WORK: The *Heroes, Hard Times, High Places*[21]

• How have you seen God's grace-at-work in the *heroes* of your story? That is, who is a person(s) you have looked up to spiritually? How have they influenced you?

• How have you seen God's grace-at-work in a *hard time* in your story? (That is, a difficult event or series of events that has profoundly marked you or changed the direction of your journey.)

• How have you seen God's grace-at-work in the *high places* of your life? (That is, moments when life seemed to really come together in a rewarding way.)

prayer

What has this reflection and conversation stirred in your mind and heart? Convert your thoughts and feelings into a written prayer:

Search me, O God, and know my heart;
Test me and know my anxious thoughts.
Point out anything in me that offends you,
and lead me along the path of everlasting life.

David
Psalm 139:23-24 (NLT)

GROWING UP TOGETHER...

In preparation for next week's conversation read and
reflect upon Ephesians 2:8-10, asking the question:
What might God want to do through my life?

What Am I To Do With My Life?

An Ephesians 2:10 Way of Life

An Ephesians 2:10
Way of Life

PREPARATION: Read and reflect upon Ephesians 2:8-10, asking the question: *What might God want to do through my life?*

——————— ⚶ ———————

What you are is God's gift to you.
What you can become is your gift to God.[22]

Henrietta Mears

The place God calls you to is the place where your deep gladness
and the world's deep hunger meet.[23]

Frederick Buechner

Lord, teach me to listen. The times are noisy and my ears are weary
with the thousand raucous sounds which continuously assault me.
Give me the spirit of the boy Samuel when he said to Thee,
"Speak, for thy servant heareth."
Let me hear Thee speaking in my heart.
Let me get used to the sound of Thy voice.[24]

A.W. Tozer

God is looking for men and women on whom He can lay a burden
without a thousand objections.

Paul Rader

——————— ⚶ ———————

reflection

In 1905 the Grand Trunk Railroad was beginning to wend its way through southeastern Saskatchewan, Canada. Along the newly laid tracks, one particular community was given the name Ituna; today it has a population of around 700. It is said that Ituna got its name because the letter "I" was next in the alphabet—the last few communities had already been named Fenwood, Goodeve and Hubbard. It is also believed that Ituna got its name from Rudyard Kipling's story "Puck of Pook's Hill." In that story, Kipling tells of a wall built by the Romans to keep out the Scots. The wall spanned what is now the English countryside from Segedunum on the east coast to Ituna on the west, and still exists today. In any event, the hard working and rugged Itunians appreciate the unique history of their town's name.

The railroad brought with it opportunity for Anglo-Saxon and Ukrainian settlers to clear the bush and squat the land with the hope of someday making a livelihood from their new farms. Purchase of the land was made official when the settlers could put up a building or two within three years and come up with the $10 to pay for their 160 acres.[25]

Many of those early farms remain in the same families that had the courage and fortitude to settle the land all those years ago. These are hard working folks who still pride themselves on an honest day's work and a type of farming that keeps the land clean. Their commitment to farming and love for the land has also brought with it a lifestyle of simplicity and frugality. All this may sound admirable, but a visit to the local coffee shop and some discreet eavesdropping would reveal a sort of tired frustration with the farming way, and a hope that someday a stroke of luck might come along—often expressed as a hope for the winning ticket in "Lotto 649." The stories of complaint turn into stories of dreaming—dreaming of what life and farming could be like if only luck would come their way.

Recently, on some of the same family farms in the Ituna area, some mining companies were given permission to perform exploratory testing for various types of mineral deposits underground. These mining prospectors soon became the brunt of some of the coffee shop conversations, which were mainly a mixture of disbelief and pride that someone from outside Ituna could tell them something new about the land they had known intimately for decades. The conversations soon headed a different direction, however, when to the utter surprise of the local farmers, diamonds were discovered on their properties by the mining prospectors.

There are seasons in our lives when, like those Ituna farmers, we find ourselves wondering, "Is this as good as it gets?" Or from time to time we may hold onto a secret wish, "If only luck would come my way." Our lives are often lived in a tension between being faithful to what we have been given to do (raise the kids, till the land, pay the bills, play when we can), and hoping for a way of life that is more true to who we hope we could someday become and what we hope we might even be able to someday do.

> **For we are what he has made us, created in Christ Jesus for good works, which God prepared beforehand to be our way of life.**
>
> *Ephesians 2:10*

In Ephesians 2:8-10, the Apostle Paul shares some "lucky" news with folks in the local community of Ephesus—news that would serve as a reminder that even in the midst of all of the good and hard work that had been done, or could be done, God had already deposited under the surface of their lives something greater.

These gracious deposits were first and foremost a *salvation* to a restored and ever-growing relationship with God—a relationship that would have implications for every aspect of their lives. And secondly, a promise of being particularly invited and expected to participate with God through *good works* which were not only to be discovered and enjoyed, but were to become *a way of life.*

54

The life I am living is not the same as the life that
wants to live in me. In those moments I sometimes
catch a glimpse of my true life,
a life hidden like the river beneath the ice.
And in the spirit of the poet, I wonder:
What am I meant to do? Who am I meant to be?[26]

Parker Palmer

It is a sad and limiting mistake to think of these *good works* as being primarily for apostles, pastors or missionaries who should be concerned with such things. This good news is good for all of us as believers in Christ. In fact, it is news we can no longer ignore. If we have moved from a *disobedient* way of life to an *obedient* one, then we have moved from a *deaf* way of living to a way of life where we are now able to *hear* more clearly the work of the Spirit of God—that already present good work that is taking place within us right now; already designed, deposited and perhaps waiting patiently to be discovered. If we can assume for a moment that God may be prone to surprise and blessing, then we would do well to become attentive to the question, "What might God want to do through my life?"—but be forewarned. Such attentiveness will most surely bring with it an alignment toward a new way of life—a *good works* sort of life as surprising as diamonds in Ituna.

conversation

Good conversation requires *deep listening* and *honest dialogue*. We invite you to continue some good conversation through the questions below. Listen for new questions and perspectives emerging from your time together. May our listening together invite a deeper understanding and appreciation for who God is, who we are, and what God desires to do through our lives.

• What stood out to you from the above reflection?

• Do you ever prayerfully wonder what the *good works* are *which God has prepared to be your way of life?* What are some of the things you wonder about?

• What areas of your life will need some attention if your *way of life* is to become aligned with those *good works*?

prayer

What has this reflection and conversation stirred in your mind and heart? Convert your thoughts and feelings into a written prayer:

Speak Lord, for your servant is listening.

I Samuel 3:9

GROWING UP TOGETHER...

In preparation for next week's conversation read and reflect upon Ephesians 2:18-22 & 4:11-16, asking the question: *How then are we to live and serve togeher?*

What Am I To Do With My Life?

A Life Together

A Life Together

PREPARATION: Read and reflect upon Ephesians 2:18-22; 4:11-16, asking the question: *How then are we to live and serve together?*

———— ❧ ————

People are longing to rediscover true community.
We have had enough of loneliness, independence, and competition.

Jean Vanier

God is building a home. He's using us all—
irrespective of how we got here—in what he is building.
He used the apostles and prophets for the foundation.
Now he's using you, fitting you in brick by brick, stone by stone,
with Christ Jesus as the cornerstone that holds all the parts together.
We see it taking shape day after day—
a holy temple built by God, all of us built into it,
a temple in which God is quite at home.

Apostle Paul
Ephesians 2:19-22
The Message

They love one another. They never fail to help widows;
they save orphans from those who would hurt them.
If they have something they give freely to the man who has nothing;
if they see a stranger, they take him home, and are happy,
as though he were a real brother.
They don't consider themselves brothers in the usual sense,
but brother instead through the Spirit, in God.[27]

Aristides describing Christians to the Emperor Hadrian
2nd Century AD

———— ❧ ————

reflection

"Spiritual growth is just too hard to maintain alone." Christian psychologist David Benner tells this story;

> A friend who was unhappy with the church had an interesting reply when I recently asked him why he continued to attend, even if intermittently. He answered that he was afraid that he would stop growing if he dropped out of church. He went on: "Even if I get nothing out of the sermon and even if I have trouble encountering God in the rest of the service, church keeps me in touch with others on the spiritual journey. Spiritual growth is just too hard to maintain alone."[28]

Benner goes on to conclude,

> The Christian spiritual journey is a journey we take with others. Each of us must take our own journey, and for each of us that journey will be unique. But none of us is intended to make that journey alone. The myth of the solitary Christian making his or her own way alone flies in the face of everything the Bible teaches about the church as the body of Christ (1 Corinthians 12:12-31)... We cannot make the journey apart from spiritual companions and community.[29]

The myth of a solitary Christian is most convincing to those of us who seek to grow up into Christ. We live in a very individualistic culture. And this culture works like a template, shaping the way we all see the world. Simply by virtue of living and breathing in this part of the world, we have encountered subtle and relentless cultural pressures that cause us to interpret our lives individually. We hold on tightly to a solitary way of seeing and being in the world. Because of this, our notions of growing up into Christ are many times just glorified self-improvement plans. This is where the gospel of Jesus confronts many of us even now. God's way challenges not just the *content* of our individual life, but also the *template*—our isolating way of thinking and living.

We must not underestimate how strongly some of these individualizing pressures stand against a life "rooted and grounded in God's love" (Ephesians 3:17), in which we are being "built together spiritually into a dwelling place for God" (Ephesians 2:22). God intends not just to transform our lives; he also intends for us to share in *his* life and work in the world. And God intends for us to do this *together*. Or, as one person has put it, God patiently matures us from a "lonely I" to a "glorious we." We humans are not the sorts of beings that flourish on our own. We are designed to love and be loved by God, and to love and be loved by our neighbors. In Ephesians 4:7-16, Paul communicates a vision of maturity that one New Testament scholar has summarized this way; "each member contributes to the growth of the body."[30] This is the mystery of how God's Spirit nurtures us as Christ's body. God's grace works *in* us, *with* us, *through* us, and *among* us. If we are to grow to maturity in Christ, we will ·do so only in the company of others. The life that God has in mind for us is truly a "life together."

One of the concrete ways in which we can learn to live this "life together" in the midst of this individualistic culture is through the practice of friendship. Spiritual friendship does not naturally grow out of the fast-paced, competitive, and isolated lives so many of us live. In reality, our professional priorities and our household busy-ness so often stand against the cultivation of deep friendship. Yet, as we pay attention to and allow space for the common sharing, honoring, and enjoying of life, something of the Spirit's nurturing grace is imparted to us.

Eugene Peterson insightfully describes our deep need these days for fellow travelers along way of following Jesus:

> *Each of us has contact with hundreds of people who never look beyond our surface appearance. We have dealings with hundreds of people who the moment they set eyes on us begin calculating what use we can be to them, what they can get out of us. We meet hundreds of people who take one look at us, make a snap judgment, and then slot us into a category so that they won't have to deal with us as persons. They treat us as something less than we are; and if we're in constant association with them, we become less.*

And then someone enters into our life who isn't looking for someone to use, is leisurely enough to find out what's really going on in us, is secure enough not to exploit our weaknesses or attack our strengths, recognizes our inner life and understands the difficulty of living out our inner convictions, confirms what is deepest within us. A friend.[31]

The tale of an individual human life is too often told as a sequence of independent and unshared moments. And our hearts cry out. We yearn to know and be known more intimately. We desire deeper, more enduring and meaningful connections. And without these sorts of friendships our good intentions for spiritual "self-improvement" will not materialize into mature lives of growing up in Christ. *"Spiritual growth is just too hard to maintain alone."*

In the 12th century classic <u>Spiritual Friendship</u>, Aelred of Rievaulx remarked, "Friendship heightens the joys of prosperity and mitigates the sorrows of adversity by dividing and sharing them. Hence, the best medicine in life is a friend." So, with whom are you traveling on this journey of growing up into Christ? Who are the people with whom you are learning to live a life together? Who are your spiritual friends?

conversation

Good conversation requires *deep listening* and *honest dialogue*. We invite you to continue some good conversation through the questions below. Listen for new questions and perspectives emerging from your time together. May our listening together invite a deeper understanding and appreciation for who God is, who we are, and what God desires to do through our lives.

• What stood out to you from the above reflection?

• What are the dangers of understanding our growing up into Christ as *merely* a self-improvement project?

• Who in your life has been like Eugene Peterson's "friend," that is, "someone who confirms what is deepest within" (pages 64-65)?

• How does your church community enhance or inhibit deep friendships? What would it look like to grow and serve together?

prayer

What has this reflection and conversation stirred in your mind and heart? Convert your thoughts and feelings into a written prayer:

Father, may you creatively convert this hunger for community
into a vocation, a calling—
a contemporary expression of the church's task
of reconciliation (2 Corinthians 5:18-21).
May our churches, that is, may we,
cultivate testimonies of friendship in our communities.
Spirit, be generous to *our life together,*
in Jesus' name.
Amen.

GROWING UP TOGETHER...

In preparation for next week's conversation read
and reflect upon Matthew 11:25-30, asking again the
question: *Where are you hearing Jesus' invitation in
your life?*

A Jesus Way of Life

A Jesus Way of Life

PREPARATION: Read and reflect upon Matthew 11:25-30 asking yourself the question: *Where are you hearing Jesus' invitation in your life?*

—————— ✑✎✑ ——————

A human being's highest achievement is to let God be able to help him.[32]

Søren Kierkegaard
(1813-1855)

God the Holy Spirit conceives and forms the life of Christ in us.
Our spirits are formed by Spirit—that is spiritual formation.

The primary language of spiritual formation is metaphorical,
with the metaphors coming from biology:
conception and birth, growth and maturity….
What is visible in men and women as we develop from infancy to maturity
has analogies to what is invisible in us as Christ is formed in us.

We commonly get interested in spiritual formation
when we realize that long after having completed our biological growth,
we are still not "grown up," not mature.
We find ourselves living lopsided, fragmented, and distracted,
lurching from impulse to stimulus or stuck in some role or function.
We find ourselves longing for a put-together life,
integrated and wise, centered and whole.
The classic word for it is holy—a holy life.[33]

Eugene Peterson

The glory of God is a fully alive human being.

Irenaeus
2nd Century AD

—————— ✑✎✑ ——————

reflection

It was a number of years ago now, when a group of fifty or so college students gathered in a residence hall to hear author Jerry Bridges speak on God's maturing work in their lives. He had already written a number of books on the spiritual life at the time, including <u>The Pursuit of Holiness</u>, <u>The Practice of Godliness</u>, and <u>Transforming Grace: Living Confidently in God's Unfailing Love.</u> But it was not his books or credentials that earned the students' respect. Bridge's combination of honesty, humility, and hopefulness gradually gained their trust throughout his talk. He spoke of God's love and grace as an experienced fellow traveler on the road of faithfulness and maturity. And the longer he spoke, the more the group seemed to trust him. At the end, he invited feedback and conversation from the students. A number of observations and comments were made, but it was one student's question that focused the remainder of the conversation.

"How do we know if we are actually growing up spiritually?" the student shouted out from the back of the residence hall lobby. This question *cut to the chase* for many of the other students. The young man spoke of how hard it was for him to have any clear sense of what God was doing generally, or even if God was doing anything more particularly in his life. He just couldn't see what God was up to amidst his current set of life circumstances. As he spoke one could sense the despair of this young man. He ended his extended question where he started; "How can I know if I am growing spiritually?"

Measuring progress in the spiritual life is a difficult and tricky endeavor. Jerry Bridges began his response with that word of caution. He discouraged any sure-fire, across the board standard of measuring spiritual maturity. We can be so easily self-deceived. He told the group that *if* he had to offer a way of judging our growth from time to time it would *not* be based on our confidence in managing sin or any felt-sense of "having really arrived" in one's relationship with God. Bridges then looked at the young man and asked, "How can you know if you are growing spiritually? The most reliable way I know is this: *Are you growing in an awareness of your need for God?"* He then proceeded to explain that it is our weakness—our sense of waywardness and need for God—that drives us throughout our lives to discover God's abundant grace and life and work.

Are we growing into an awareness of our need for God?

Jesus' life intersected with peoples' deep awareness of need wherever he traveled. He both identified people and drew them to a place of longing and mercy. Matthew records one scene where Jesus prays;

> *"O Father, Lord of heaven and earth, thank you for hiding the truth from those who think themselves so wise and clever, and for revealing it to the childlike. Yes, Father, it pleased you to do it this way!*
>
> *"My Father has given me authority over everything. No one really knows the Son except the Father, and no one really knows the Father except the Son and those to whom the Son chooses to reveal him."*
>
> *Then Jesus said, "Come to me, all of you who are weary and carry heavy burdens, and I will give you rest. Take my yoke upon you. Let me teach you, because I am humble and gentle, and you will find rest for your souls. For my yoke fits perfectly, and the burden I give you is light." (Matthew 11:25-30, NLT)*

Jesus' invitation to *"Come....Take my yoke....Let me teach you"* still resonates through the sighs and decisions and needs of our lives and communities today, just as it did then. And Jesus' lessons are never independent of his person. Many of us are weary. Many of us carry heavy burdens. Do we hear over and over again Jesus' gentle invitation to join him in his way of life?

We cannot simply reach out and grasp such a way of life. There is no simple solution that can be purchased or picked off the shelf. We cannot read it in a manual and then simply follow the directions. Rather, this sort of prayerful life demands that we immerse ourselves in a relationship of learning with Jesus. "Come...Take my yoke...Let me teach you." The greatest privilege we can have in our spiritual lives is to have a sense of our need for God. When we lose our sense of need we find ourselves deaf to Jesus' invitation to join him in his way of life.

The eight conversations in <u>Growing Up</u> have invited you to consider three primary questions for your journey: "Who is God?" "Who am I?" "What am I to do with my life?" We never grow out of these questions along the way of following Jesus—we grow into them. Our hope has been that these past several weeks have served to deepen your attentiveness and responsiveness to God's gracious and maturing work in the world, in your community, and in your life.

> Are we growing into an awareness of our need for God?

So, what happens now? What do you need next on this journey of growing up into Christ? In the reality of your life, how are you hearing Jesus' gracious invitation to *come* and *learn from him* and *join him in his way of life*?

conversation

Good conversation requires *deep listening* and *honest dialogue*. We invite you to continue some good conversation through the questions below. Listen for new questions and perspectives emerging from your time together. May our listening together invite a deeper understanding and appreciation for who God is, who we are, and what God desires to do through our lives.

• What stood out to you from the above reflection?

• Throughout the past seven weeks we have encouraged you in each conversation to convert your thoughts and feelings into a written prayer. Look back through the conversations. What are the prayers that you have found yourself praying over the past few weeks? What themes have emerged?

- What do *you* need next on the journey?

- How can we pray for each other?

prayer

What has this reflection and conversation stirred in your mind and heart? Convert your thoughts and feelings into a written prayer of commitment:

O God,
rouse us to thanksgiving
because we belong to your family.
Wake the sleeper in us
and kindle such a fire in our hearts
that we may never be content
with anything short of you.
Relight in us the flame
of a steady life of prayer.
O God,
Keep open our minds, our souls, our hearts.
Amen.[34]

Endnotes:

[1] St. Augustine, <u>Confessions</u>, trans. Henry Chadwick, (Oxford, England: Oxford University Press, 1991), 3.

[2] Quoted by Siang-Yang Tan, <u>Full Service</u>, (Grand Rapids, MI: Baker Books, 2006), 135.

[3] Luci Shaw, <u>Water My Soul: Cultivating the Interior Life</u>, (Vancouver, B.C.: Regent College Publishing, 2003), 48-49.

[4] John Ortberg, <u>The Life You've Always Wanted</u>, (Grand Rapids, MI: Zondervan, 1997), 17.

[5] Alister McGrath, <u>The Journey: A Pilgrim in the Lands of the Spirit</u>, (New York, NY: Doubleday, 1999), 3.

[6] J.I. Packer, <u>Knowing God</u>, (Downers Grove, IL: IVP, 1973), 11-12.

[7] Eugene Peterson, <u>Leap Over A Wall</u>, (San Francisco, CA: HarperCollins, 1997), 207.

[8] Edwin Searcy, ed., <u>Awed to Heaven, Rooted in Earth: Prayers of Walter Brueggeman</u>, (Minneapolis, MN: Fortress Press, 2003), 55.

[9] C.S. Lewis, <u>Mere Christianity</u>, (San Francisco, CA: HarperCollins, 2001 edition), 177.

[10] Debra Rienstra, <u>So Much More: An Invitation to Christian Spirituality</u>, (San Francisco, CA: Jossey-Bass, 2005), 62.

[11] Peter van Breemen, <u>The God Who Won't Let Go</u>, (Notre Dame, IN: Ave Maria Press, 2001), 19.

[12] David Benner, <u>The Gift of Being Yourself: The Sacred Call of Self-Discovery</u>, (Downers Grove, IL: IVP, 2004), 47.

[13] Desmond Tutu, <u>God Has A Dream: A Vision of Hope For Our Time</u>, (New York, NY: Doubleday, 2004), 32.

[14] Dietrich Bonhoeffer, poem appeared in *Christianity & Crisis*, March 4, 1946.

[15] Quoted by James M. Houston, <u>The Disciple: Following The True Mentor</u>, (Colorado Springs, CO: David C Cook, 2007), 14.

[16] Donald K. McKim, editor, <u>Calvin's Institutes: Abridged Edition</u>, (Louisville, KY: Westminister John Knox Press, 2001), 1.

[17] Anne Lamott, <u>Traveling Mercies: Some Thoughts on Faith</u>, (New York, NY: Anchor Books, 1999), 139.

[18] Christian author Daniel Taylor writes, "Seeing our lives as stories is more than a powerful metaphor. It is how experience presents itself to us. By better understanding story, and our role as characters, we can live more purposefully the kind of life that will give our own story meaning." Daniel Taylor, <u>Tell Me A Story: The Life-Shaping Power of Our Stories,</u> (St. Paul, MN: Bog Walk Press, 2001), 3-4.

[19] John Eldredge, <u>Epic: The Story God is Telling and the Role That Is Yours To Play</u>, (Nashville, TN: Thomas Nelson, 2004), 5-7.

[20] Eugene Peterson, <u>The Contemplative Pastor</u>, (Grand Rapids, MI: Eerdmans, 1989), 4.

[21] This framework of heroes, hard times, and high places was introduced by Lesa Engelthaler "Good Mentoring" in <u>Leadership Journal</u>, Vol. 27, Issue 3, Summer 2006.

[22] Earl Roe, <u>Dream Big, The Henrietta Mears Story</u>, (Ventura, CA: Regal Books, 1990), 20.

[23] Frederick, Buechner, <u>Listening to Your Life: Daily Meditations with Frederick Buechner</u>, (San Francisco, CA: Harper Collins, 1992), 186.

[24] Quoted by John Eldredge, <u>The Sacred Romance Workbook and Journal</u>, (Nashville, TN: Thomas Nelson, 2000), 31.

[25] Historical information on the town of Ituna, Saskatchewan used from the website, www.town.ituna.sk.ca/History.html, 2007.

[26] Parker Palmer, <u>Let Your Life Speak</u>, (San Francisco, CA: Jossey-Bass, 2000), 2.

[27] Charles Colson, <u>Loving God</u>, (Grand Rapids, MI: Brazos Press, 2002), 41.

[28] David Benner, <u>Sacred Companions: The Gift of Spiritual Friendship & Direction</u>, (Downers Grove, IL: IVP, 2002), 39-40.

[29] Benner, <u>Sacred Companions: The Gift of Spiritual Friendship & Direction</u>, 40.

[30] Clinton E. Arnold, Frank S. Thielman, S.M. Baugh, <u>Zondervan Illustrated Bible Backgrounds Commentary: Ephesians Philippians Colossians Philemon</u>, (Grand Rapids, MI: Zondervan, 2002), 26.

[31] Eugene Peterson, <u>Leap over a Wall</u>, (San Francisco, CA: Harper Collins, 1997), 54.

[32] Quoted by James M. Houston, <u>The Disciple: Following The True Mentor</u>, (Colorado Springs, CO: David C Cook, 2007), 14.

[33] Eugene Peterson, <u>Take Up and Read, Spiritual Reading: An Annotated List</u>, (Grand Rapids, MI: Eerdmans, 1996), 32-33.

[34] Taken from Don Postema, <u>Space for God: A Leader's Guide</u>, (Grand Rapids, MI: CRC Publications, 1983), 25.

**Portions of *Conversation One* were adapted from "The gift of being a growing person," *Fragments* (April 30, 2003); portions of *Conversation Three* were adapted from "A reflection on Ephesians 2:1-10," *Fragments* (January 15, 2004); portions of *Conversation Seven* were adapted from "Some Thoughts on Friendship," *Fragments* (December 27, 2001). With permission from the Joshua Foundation For Christian Mentoring (www.jfcm.com).

Our Ephesians 2:10 Story

Along a 210-Freeway morning commute to Pasadena, California in the spring of 1996, a seed was planted which would grow into work of VANTAGEPOINT[3]. As Randy Reese sat in Los Angeles traffic that spring morning, he considered the legacies of Charles Simeon (1759-1836) and Henrietta Mears (1890-1963). Both people had brought significant depth and renewal to the Church and both had paid careful attention to the leadership development of others. While pondering their lives that morning, Randy's heart was grabbed by the Apostle Paul's words in Ephesians 2:10; "For we are what he has made us, created in Christ Jesus for good works, which he prepared beforehand to be our way of life." He sensed the Lord inviting him to participate in a similar movement as Simeon and Mears, a movement of fostering depth and renewal in the Church through the discipleship of others as Christian leaders.

This seed has grown and we at VP3 today are so grateful for the ways in which our lives and work have intersected with so many of yours. We count it an honor to share in a small way in your ongoing journey of discovering more deeply who God is, who you are in Christ, and the good works, which God prepared beforehand to be your way of life.